Praise for *Cannonball In*

"*Cannonball In* is a brilliant story that will resonate with children and adults alike, for its message of overcoming fear and celebrating our uniqueness is universal. Beautifully written and illustrated, the book is one that you will want to read again and again, and each time you will want to stand and cheer. Tara Martin is known for her genuine spirit, and her words flow onto the page in a way that will speak directly to your heart. *Cannonball In* will surely make waves!"

—**Kim Bearden**, cofounder of the Ron Clark Academy, author of *Talk to Me*

"*Cannonball In* is a sensitive recounting of a special relationship between father and child, accompanied by engaging illustrations that flow delicately with the theme. I would choose this title for a library, for a child's home collection, or as a special gift for a grandchild! *Cannonball In* would make an engaging and meaningful read-aloud. Embedded in the story are two important and timely life messages: 1) It is okay if you don't look like your parents, and 2) you can find the courage to take on the unknown. I hope this will be the first of more works to come from this author."

—**Dr. Mary Devin**, university professor of educational leadership, former teacher, director of school libraries, superintendent, parent, grandparent

"*Cannonball In* is a heartwarming story of bravery, perseverance, and kindness. Tara Martin does a phenomenal job of bringing her characters to life with each turn of the page. This book is perfect for children and adults of all ages and would be a wonderful addition to any school library. Thank you, Tara, for helping us to make a splash and find our purpose, passion, and courage."

—**Beth Houf**, proud principal and author of *Lead Like a Pirate*

"Life is about not living in fear of what others may think and say; life is about living life to the fullest! We are meant to live purposefully and passionately, working to be the best version of ourselves. Tara's beautiful children's book nails this!"

—**Hamish Brewer**, relentless, tattooed, skateboarding principal

"Today's society seeks guidance, wisdom, and encouragement for living. I've seen this over the years, not only as an educator, leader, mentor, and entrepreneur but most importantly as a father. As I read the pages, I reflected on those precious moments when it was important to know my own identity and for my daughter to know hers as well. *Cannonball In* explores our identities and the spirit inside of us in a way that will warm the heart, feed the soul, and provide a sense of triumph, victory, and joy. As someone who has mentored many over the years, I can say without hesitation that this book will speak to the hearts and minds of many across all ages, ethnicities, and cultures. *Cannonball In* is about you, me, and all of us recognizing and affirming the greatness within. Get this book and begin to refresh and renew the greatness within you and all whom you influence."

—**Vernon Wright**, leader, show host of #TheManyVoicesOfGrit, mentor, and founder, The Wright Leader LLC

"Having read thousands of picture books over the years, *Cannonball In* has very quickly risen to the top of my list. It's a story all kids and adults can relate to, with such a powerful message we can all teach. You'll face your fears, find your true friends, and never look back!"

—**Adam Welcome**, author, speaker, educator, picture book fanatic

Cannonball In

PACIFIC ACADEMY MIDDLE SCHOOL
10238 - 168 Street
Surrey, B.C.
V4N 1Z4

Tara Martin

Illustrated by Genesis Kohler

Cannonball In

© 2019 by Tara Martin

All rights reserved. No part of this publication may be reproduced in any form or by any electronic or mechanical means, including information storage and retrieval systems, without permission in writing by the publisher, except by a reviewer who may quote brief passages in a review. For information regarding permission, contact the publisher at books@daveburgessconsulting.com.

>This book is available at special discounts when purchased in quantity for use as premiums, promotions, fundraisers, or for educational use. For inquiries and details, contact the publisher at books@daveburgessconsulting.com.

>For more books from Dave Burgess Consulting, Inc.,
>visit DaveBurgessConsulting.com/dbcibooks.

Published by Dave Burgess Consulting, Inc. San Diego, CA
DaveBurgessConsulting.com

Cover Design and Illustrations by Genesis Kohler
Editing and Interior Design by My Writers' Connection

Library of Congress Control Number: 2019944964
Paperback ISBN: 978-1-949595-64-2
Hardback ISBN: 978-1-949595-65-9

First Printing: August 2019

This book is dedicated to my sweet boy, Kaleb Martin, who is becoming a man right before my eyes.

Kaleb, don't let the fear of doubt paralyze you from chasing your dreams and ambitions.

This world needs YOU to make a splash, buddy!

Cannonball In!

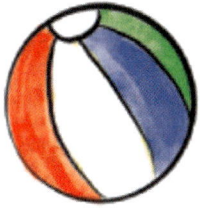

Olivia's dad had trained her well. She had become quite the confident swimmer—in the shallow end of the city pool, that is.

She longed to join the jumpers.

Some dove like dolphins.

Then there were the gymnast jumpers, the flippers.

Others ran and jumped without thinking twice about technique or form.

But Olivia's favorite jumpers of all time were the cannonballers. Sometimes their splashes reached her all the way at the shallow end!

Those jumpers make waves! I want to make waves like that one day, she thought.

"Olivia, when are you going to jump?" Dad asked.

She looked up at him and whispered, "I'm too scared, Dad. I can't touch the bottom if I need to come up for air."

"You don't need to touch the bottom. You can swim," Dad said.

"Take my hand; I'll go with you. Today is your day to cannonball in."

Her dad went first, and Olivia focused on his every move.

"Climb the ladder with purpose!

"Then run, jump, grab both legs, and make your splash!" he said.

And he did! Dad made cannonballing in look so simple. The massive waves he made soaked the lifeguards every single time!

It's my turn, Olivia thought, heart pounding.

She climbed the ladder with purpose—sort of.

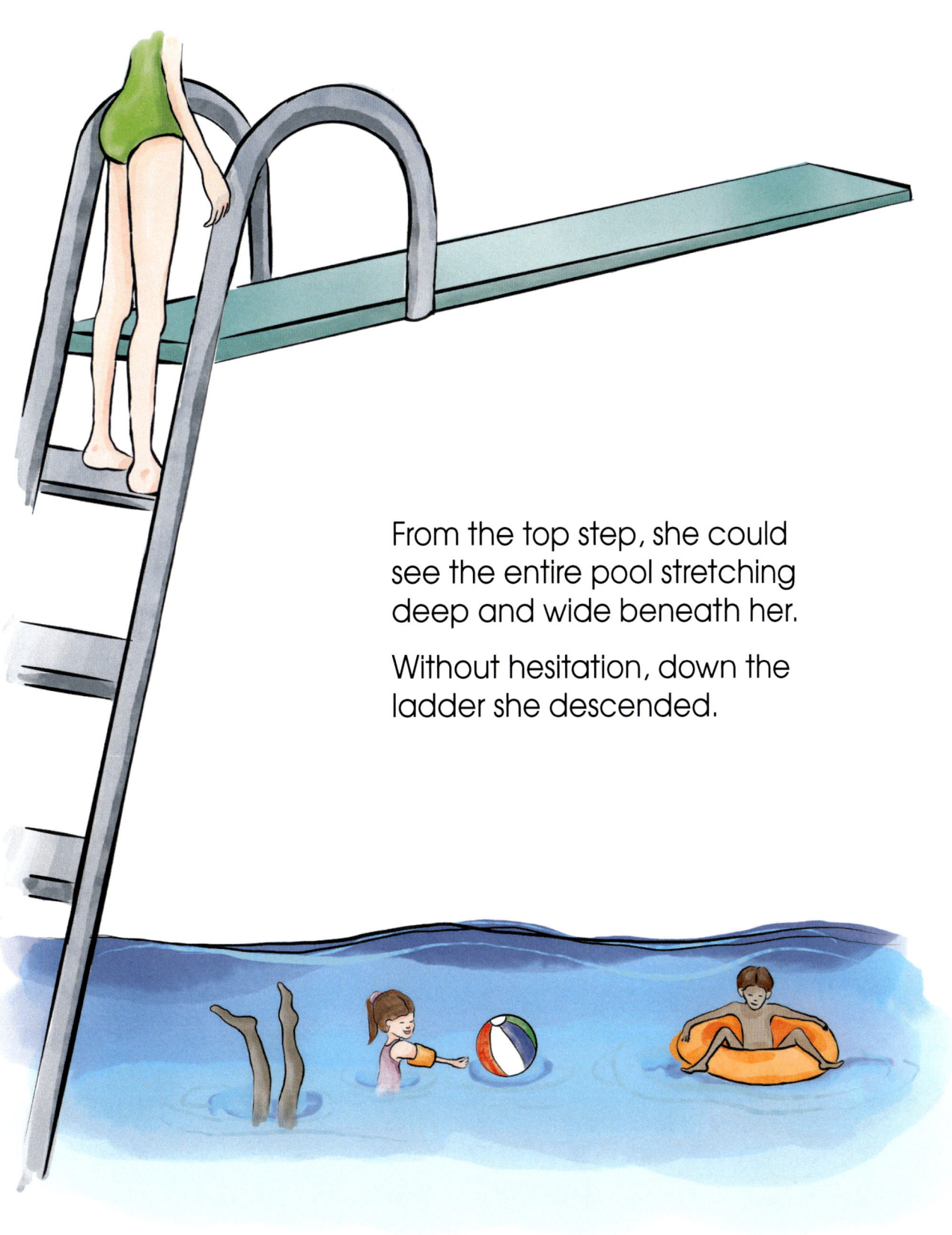

From the top step, she could see the entire pool stretching deep and wide beneath her.

Without hesitation, down the ladder she descended.

As her feet met the steamy, hot concrete, her head hung in shame. Olivia never looked up as she walked past the dabblers who sat on the side of the pool, but she couldn't ignore their words.

"What a wimp!" one cried out.

"Chicken!" another said, adding a cluck.

Her dad met her before she made it to the shallow end of the pool. "Olivia, you want to jump in, right?" he asked tenderly.

"Yes, Dad. I do. I'm sorry I let you down. I want to cannonball in. Deep down, I do."

"Then it's your time. Go! Make your splash!"

After waiting for what seemed like an eternity for her turn, Olivia climbed that ladder with purpose (for real this time) and refused to listen to the calls of "chicken" that came from the children in line behind her.

Once she reached the board, she made a running start and never looked back.

Olivia sprung from the board, grabbed both knees and pulled them close to her chest, just as she had seen performed so many times.

This is it! I'm going to make waves! she thought as she flew through the air.

Crash! Splash!

Then down and down she sank. She stretched out her feet to touch the bottom but felt nothing but water beneath her.

At that moment, she could feel her pulse in her temples from the water pressure, and she almost panicked. In her mind, she heard her dad's words, "You know how to swim. You KNOW how to swim."

At that thought, she looked up and focused on the sunlight beaming through the water and swam—just as she had done time after time in the shallow end.

With each stroke,

She pushed doubt behind her.

She pushed fear behind her.

She pushed "I can't" behind her.

She pushed "What if my splash wasn't good enough?" behind her.

And she swam!

With shortness of breath, Olivia climbed out of the pool. As she looked back at the ripples on the water's surface left by her jump, she smiled and thought, *I did that!*

This time, as she walked past the dabblers, she held her head high, feeling proud. She nodded and smiled, and in return one of them snarked, "Is that all you have, Twiggy?"

"What kind of splash is that?" asked another.

"When you hit the water, you got a wedgie; we saw your behind from here!"

Olivia's smile quickly faded. Each insult felt like an arrow ablaze, piercing her mind and heart. Her courage had been singed.

Rather than getting back in line for another jump, she made her way to the shallow end of the pool–her safe zone.

"Where are you going?" Dad asked, stopping Olivia in her tracks.

"Did you hear them, Dad? My splash was small, and they saw my bottom!"

"Listen to me," he said adamantly, "the dabblers are not jumping. They have dry hair; they are not even wet! Their opinion of jumpers does not matter. Besides, what do they know about jumping if they are not in the water, Olivia?"

"You cannonballed in! You pushed fear and doubt behind you. You swam! You did that, Olivia!

"You were not born to sit on the sidelines and watch others make a splash.

"You were born to jump!"

Olivia's courage began to swell up inside as her father spoke. She gave him a squeezy hug and said, "Thanks, Dad."

As she headed back to the diving board, a couple of kids swam to the edge of the pool and called up to her. "Hey, that was the best cannonball ever! We saw it from here!" the girl said.

Olivia couldn't believe her ears and thought,

My ripples?

The best cannonball ever?

For real?

"I wish I could jump like that, but I'm too scared. I can't touch the bottom over there!" chimed in the little boy.

"But you can both swim?" Olivia asked.

"Like fish in the sea," the little girl replied.

Olivia grinned and said, "Take my hand. I'll go with you. Today is the day! Let's cannonball in!"

As Olivia's dad watched his daughter lead the kids hand in hand toward the diving board, he beamed from within and whispered proudly, "Now *that* is what you were born to do!"

A Note from the Author

This book is based on a true story; it's one of my favorite memories with my dad—not biological, but the one who raised me. My dad's grandmother was Cherokee. Therefore, the illustrations within *Cannonball In* represent my childhood reality. I believe the message of *Cannonball In* is fitting for all people of all backgrounds, and I want the readers to relate in a real way through the words and the illustrations.

My dad instilled in me a *Cannonball In* mindset that I have embraced throughout life. Not only do I jump in on opportunities life offers me, but I have the honor of encouraging those I serve to go *all-in* on their ideas too. Therefore, the end of the story comes full circle to convey this message.

Cannonball in!

Acknowledgments

I want to thank my God for keeping watch over me through all my *Cannonball In* adventures in this thing called life. That's a tough job!

To my guys, Darrell and Kaleb. You two have my heart, and I adore how we stretch each other to chase our dreams and ambitions. I love y'all so much!

Dave and Shelley Burgess, thank you for taking a chance on this redhead in Kansas! Your leadership and mentoring have encouraged me to go *all in* many, many times. You two mean more to me than words alone can express. I appreciate you!

To my illustrator, Genesis Kohler, your talent astounds me, friend! You truly made my words come alive, and I'm forever grateful! *(I'm still gushing over these illustrations; for REAL!)* Keep blessing the world with your beautiful gift!

To my deceased stepdad, thank you for teaching me the *Cannonball In* mindset years ago. I think you'd be proud to know I'm still making a splash!

To my family and extended family, thank you for the real experiences that have helped mold me into the vessel needed to serve my purpose in this world.

To all students within my realm of influence and beyond, don't fear the unknown! Follow your dreams and make *your* splash!

To all of my fellow educators, mentors, and leaders who have taught me so much along this journey, I appreciate you. We are truly better together.

To my PLFamily—you guys stretch me to *Cannonball In* and grow as an educator **every** single day. I'm grateful to be connected.

To my astounding book team—Erin, you and your team are outstanding! None of this would have been possible without you all.

If you have a heartbeat, this one is for *you*! Don't let the fear of doubt paralyze you. *Cannonball In!* Embrace your full potential. Today is your day!

About the Author

Tara Martin is an enthusiastic educator, speaker, and author of *Be REAL: Educate from the Heart*. Tara thrives on change and refuses to settle for the status quo. She has served as a classroom teacher, an instructional coach, a district administrator, and the director of media and communications for Dave Burgess Consulting, Inc. As the founder of #BookSnaps, she is always seeking unique ways to make learning fun, relevant, and meaningful.

Tara's ambition is to lead a culture of innovative change and encourage others to Cannonball In and fulfill their true potential—professionally and personally!

A Little More About the Author

Tara is a mom and wife who lives on a Kansas farm with no animals. She loves writing, shopping, ice cream, art museums, flexing, giggling, and traveling. She is a dreamer and is always *Cannonballing In* on her ideas and ambitions!

Connect with Tara
Twitter: @TaraMartinEDU
Book Resources: tarammartin.com/cannonballin

About the Illustrator

Genesis Kohler earned a BFA at the Herron School of Art in Indianapolis, Indiana. She lives in the west of Ireland with her husband and son and their cat, *Faoiste* (Fwee-shta, which means "fudge" in Irish). When she isn't creating art or reading, she tends to take way too many pictures of sheep.

PACIFIC ACADEMY MIDDLE SCHOOL
10238 - 168 Street
Surrey, B.C.
V4N 1Z4

Manufactured by Amazon.ca
Bolton, ON